you are awesome.

This edition first published in Great Britain in 2024
by SJG Gift Publishing, HP22 6NE.

All rights reserved. No part of this work may be reproduced in any form or by any means, electronic or mechanical, including photocopying, recording or by any information storage and retrieval system, without the prior written permission of the publisher.

All information in this publication is for educational and informational purposes. It is not intended as a substitute for professional advice. Should you decide to act upon any information in this publication, you do so at your own risk. While the information in this publication has been verified to the best of our abilities, we cannot guarantee that there are no mistakes or errors.

© Susanna Geoghegan Gift Publishing

Author: Sasha Morton
Design: Bag of Badgers Ltd.

ISBN: 978-1-915902-68-9

Printed in China

10 9 8 7 6 5 4 3 2 1

Welcome to **You Are Awesome** – a collection of **empowering, inclusive and life-affirming** words of advice about knowing your own value and **never doubting yourself**. With uplifting and meaningful quotes and mantras to promote self-worth, confidence and optimism, these speakers will encourage you to celebrate yourself, your values and your place in the world. It's time to own being the brilliant, unique and awesome person that you are! **Enjoy!**

> Be happy with being you.
> Love your flaws.
> Own your quirks.
> And know that you are just as perfect as anyone else, exactly as you are.

Ariana Grande

You can be **great** just by being yourself.

Steven Spielberg

In order to be irreplaceable, one must always be different.

Coco Chanel

> You only live once, but if you do it right, once is enough.

Mae West

> The single most powerful thing I can be is to **be myself**.

Dwayne 'The Rock' Johnson

> I just make it my business to get along with people so I **can have fun**. It's that simple.

Betty White

> As long as you keep going, you'll keep getting better. And as you get better, you gain more confidence. That alone is **SUCCESS.**

Tamara Taylor

> I don't believe makeup and the right hairstyle alone can make a woman beautiful.
>
> The most radiant woman in the room is the one full of **life and experience**.

Sharon Stone

So, remember to **LOOK UP AT THE STARS AND NOT DOWN AT YOUR FEET.** Try to make sense of what you see and hold on to that childlike wonder about what makes the universe exist.

Stephen Hawking

> **If what you do interests you, at least one person is pleased.**

Katherine Hepburn

I know I made
a lot of mistakes,
but they

> in turn

> > were my
> > life lessons.

Drew Barrymore

Being powerful is so much more interesting than **being beautiful.**

Helen Mirren

> Don't wait around for someone else to tell your story. Do it yourself by whatever means necessary.

— Lena Dunham

> I may not be **perfect**, but I'm **always** me.
>
> Selena Gomez

DIFFERENT IS GOOD. When someone tells you that you are different, hold your head up and be proud.

Angelina Jolie

> I'm a big believer in accepting yourself the way you are and not really worrying about it.

Jennifer Lawrence

> Don't hide your scars.
>
> They make you who you are.

Frank Sinatra

I'm a person who gets better with practice.

Getting older is awesome – because you get more practice.

Zooey Deschanel

Find out who you are and **DO IT ON PURPOSE.**

Dolly Parton

> It is never too late to be what you might have been.

George Eliot

YOU CAN BE EVERYTHING. You can be the infinite amount of things that people are.

Kesha

> It's always better to shock people and change people's expectations than to give them exactly what they think you can do.

Jonah Hill

> My mother thinks **I am the best.** And I was raised to **always believe** what my mother tells me.
>
> Diego Maradona

Promise me you'll always remember: You're braver than you believe, and stronger than you seem, and smarter than you think.

Unknown

> I think the **older you get,** the more you become your **true, essential self.**

Tom Ford

Positive thinking will let you use the ability which you have, and that is AWESOME.

Zig Ziglar

I always prefer to
believe the best
of everybody.

It saves
so much
trouble.

Rudyard Kipling

I say
I am
stronger
than fear.

Malala Yousafzai

I'm an early riser.
I work out really hard.
I push myself;
I get my job done,
and at the end of the
day, there's a **Guinness**
waiting for me.

Jason Momoa

BEING NICE IS AWESOME. You have more fun; you meet more people.

Charli XCX

I truly believe that the **privilege of a lifetime** is being who you are.

Viola Davis

> I'm not the next Usain Bolt or Michael Phelps – I'm the first **Simone Biles**.

Simone Biles

Emotions are like passing storms, and you have to remind yourself that it won't rain forever. You just have to sit down and watch it pour outside and then peek your head out when it looks dry.

Amy Poehler

Confidence
is ten percent
hard work
and
ninety percent
delusion.

Tina Fey

The world always seems **brighter** when you've just made something that wasn't there before.

Neil Gaiman

> When you love and accept yourself, when you know who really cares about you, and when you learn from your mistakes, then **you stop caring** about **what people** who **don't know you** think.

Beyoncé

> I believe one person **can** make a difference.

Greta Thunberg

If you're going to do a job, do it right.

If you're going to throw a birthday party, make it amazing.

If you're going to do anything, do it awesome.

Jimmy John Liataud

> I consider myself to be a **geniu**s who happens to play chess.

— Bobby Fischer

No one can make you feel inferior without your consent.

Eleanor Roosevelt

It's better to be
A LION FOR A DAY
than a
**SHEEP
ALL YOUR LIFE.**

Elizabeth Kenny

> A smile is a curve that sets everything straight.
>
> Phyllis Diller

When I lay my head on the pillow at night, I can say I was a **decent person** today.

That's when I feel **BEAUTIFUL**.

Drew Barrymore

No matter what a woman looks like, if she's confident, SHE'S SEXY.

Paris Hilton

Someone said **adversity builds character**, but someone else said **adversity reveals character**. I'm pleasantly surprised with my resilience. I persevere, and not just blindly. I take the best, get rid of the rest, and move on, realizing that you can make a choice to take the good.

Brooke Shields

Attitude is everything.

Diane von Furstenberg

> My legacy is that I stayed on course ... from the beginning to the end, because I believed in something inside of me.

Tina Turner

> Being cool is being your own self, not doing something that someone else is telling you to do.

Vanessa Hudgens

Loving oneself isn't hard, when you understand who and what 'yourself' is. It has nothing to do with the shape of your face, the size of your eyes, the length of your hair or the quality of your clothes. It's so beyond all of those things and it's what gives life to everything about you. Your own self is such a treasure.

Phylicia Rashad

I'M NOT A DOWNTRODDEN WOMAN.
I JUST WON'T BE.

Paloma Faith

I'd tell my 20-year-old self, 'Don't be afraid to do it all. Whatever you're interested in, just go for it. Don't wait around for a better time.'

Angela Bassett

<u>Don't</u> let that pesky low self-esteem creep in and fool you into believing that you don't have value.

<u>Don't</u> allow it to crush your will or dampen your spirit.

Gabrielle Union

If I could go back in time and tell my 10-year-old-self anything, I would tell her: Don't worry about what other people think, or about whether you're doing what they think is the right thing. The things you worry about now, they mostly won't matter. So just follow your heart.

Melissa McCarthy

> There will be parts of your body that you are not fond of.
>
> That's OK.
>
> You can love those parts of you even if you don't like them.

Tracee Ellis Ross

Enjoy yourself
a little more.
Be less
image conscious.
Learn
to relax.

Victoria Beckham

Remember who you always were, where you came from, who your parents were, how they raised you. Because that authentic self is going to follow you all through life, so make sure that it's solid so it's something that you can hold on and be proud of for the rest of your life.

Michelle Obama

Try not to live up to everyone else's expectations of yourself.

Khloe Kardashian

> I was raised to be an independent woman, **not the victim of anything.**

Kamala Harris

> **Stay true to your own voice, and don't worry about needing to be liked or what anybody else thinks. Keep your eyes on your own paper.**

Laura Dern

This is a long, long, faraway goal, but 2036 I am running for office to be president of the United States.

So, you can put that in your iCloud calendar.

Amanda Gorman

> Why should I dislike anything about my appearance?
>
> I came off the factory line this way.
>
> **I AM PERFECT.**

Shonda Rhimes

> The tragedy about this whole image-obsessed society is that young girls get so caught up in just achieving that they forget to realize that they have so much more to offer the world.

— America Ferrera

HAPPINESS AND CONFIDENCE are the **prettiest things you can wear.**

Taylor Swift

I believe in a glamorous life, and I live a glamorous life.

Lady Gaga

I'm <u>not</u> offended by blonde jokes because I know I'm not dumb … **and I also know that I'm <u>not</u> blonde.**

Dolly Parton

Once you accept that we're all **imperfect**, it's the most **liberating thing in the world**. Then you can go around making mistakes and saying the wrong thing and tripping over on the street and all that and not feel worried.

Paloma Faith

> We are all **beautiful, amazing** humans that are worthy of **love, kindness** whether that's from ourselves or other people.

Ferne Cotton

> Don't waste so much time thinking about how much you weigh. There is no more mind-numbing, boring, idiotic, self-destructive diversion from the fun of living.

Meryl Streep

I choose to take care of myself because I want to, not to prove anything to anyone.

Selena Gomez

I don't have to prove anything to anyone, I only have to follow my heart and concentrate on what I want to say to the world. **I run my world.**

Beyoncé

> One is never over-dressed or under-dressed with a Little Black Dress.

Karl Lagerfeld

STYLE
is a way to say
who you are
**without having
to speak.**

Rachel Zoe

I'm from a nice, suburban, middle-class family, but my tattoos remind me where I've been.

Tom Hardy

When a woman says, 'I have nothing to wear!', what she really means is, 'There's nothing here for who I'm supposed to be today.'

Caitlin Moran

> Bodies change. Bodies grow. Bodies shrink. It's all love (don't let anyone tell you otherwise).

Anne Hathaway

Rather than step on the scale, look at yourself in the mirror and be like,

'Dammmm girrrrrl … you're smart and talented and accomplished and perfect just the way you are.'

Rebel Wilson

The most courageous act is still to think for yourself. ALOUD.

Coco Chanel

> My body listens to me. Identify the weaknesses, shut them in a box, find your strengths, run with them.

Priyanka Chopra Jonas

I feel myself becoming the fearless person I have dreamt of being. **Have I arrived? No.** But I'm constantly evolving and challenging myself to be unafraid to make mistakes.

Janelle Monae

First they **ignore you**, then they **laugh at you**, then they **fight you**, then **you win.**

Gandhi

Oh, how I regret not having worn a bikini for the entire year I was 26. If anyone young is reading this, go, right this minute, put on a bikini, and don't take it off until you're 34.

Nora Ephron

Don't be into trends. Don't make fashion own you, **but you decide what you are,** what you want to express by the way you dress **and the way you live.**

Gianni Versace

> The minute you learn to love **yourself** you won't want to be **anyone else.**
>
> Rihanna

<u>Nobody</u> is perfect.
I just don't believe
in perfection.
But I do believe in saying,

'This is who I am
and look at me
not being perfect'.

I'M PROUD OF THAT.

Kate Winslet

Style is knowing who you are, what you want to say and not giving a damn.

Orson Welles

> I don't believe in fashion. I believe in costume. Life is too short to be the same person every day.

Stephanie Perkins

You've got to love yourself first.

> You've got to be OK on your own before you can be OK with somebody else.

You've got to value yourself and know that you're worth everything.

Jennifer Lopez

> I believe that when you put a smile out there, you get a smile back.

Heidi Klum

I like to refer to my small social circle as **'boutique.'** And much like the hotels of the same ilk, my friends are **all** unique, **high quality, and serve me good food**. But more than that, they teach me things about the world and about myself that I couldn't learn anywhere else.

Dan Levy

> You gotta have style.
> It helps you get down
> the stairs.
> It helps you get up
> in the morning.
> It's a way of life.
> Without it,
> you're nobody.

Diana Vreeland

If you can do what you do best and be happy, you're further along in life than most people.

Leonardo DiCaprio

> I've chosen to treat my life more like **a party** than something to stress **about**.

Martin Short

Once you figure out who you are and what you love about yourself, I think it all kinda falls into place.

Jennifer Aniston

Beauty comes from a life well lived. If you've lived well, your smile lines are in the right places, and your frown lines aren't too bad, what more do you need?

Jennifer Garner

Don't you ever let a soul in the world tell you that you can't be exactly who you are.

Lady Gaga

Never allow someone to be your priority while allowing yourself to be their option.

Mark Twain

I am my
>   **own muse,**
the subject
>   **I know best.**

Frida Kahlo

There are no captions on red-carpet photos that say,

'This girl trained for two weeks, she went on a juice diet, she has a professional hair and makeup person, and this dress was made for her.'

I just wish they'd say,

'It ain't the truth.'

Emilia Clarke

I DON'T REALLY GO WITH THE CROWD. I'm the kind of person that if I heard some girls were bullying my friend in another school, I would go to that school by myself and try to have a fight with a hundred girls.

Michaela Coel

It will always be **relevant** and always be **inspiring** to see somebody turning themselves into a **warrior**.

Phoebe Waller–Bridge

It only took 45 years to find myself.

Right where I am supposed to be.

And it's not perfect.

But it's me.

Drew Barrymore

When you learn to appreciate and love everything in you, **that's when you'll be most beautiful.**

Sandra Bullock

> **It's OK to be proud of hard-earned success.**
>
> **There is no shame in being a boss.**

Katy Perry

I've had a lot of voices tell me what I should be making. Personally, I would much rather live and die by my own hand. If my stuff sucks, then at least I made it suck. I didn't allow some person, some old dude in a suit, to make it suck for me.

Zendaya

> **Stop wearing your wishbone where your backbone ought to be.**
>
> — Elizabeth Gilbert

You really are good enough.
Look at your achievements.
You have done the most incredible things.
It is good to be ambitious but give yourself a break and a little pat on the back, because we have done amazing things.

Melanie C

It's OK to feel crappy sometimes and it's OK to feel like you don't look like the next person. But what you have to know is that you are beautiful, and you are strong, and you are worth it. It's important to know that.

Jordin Sparks

> You reach a certain point and you realize every person is completely different, so there's no point in comparing yourself to other people.

Nina Dobrev

> I'm my own work of art.
>
> — Madonna

Take care of yourself now that you're old enough to know how.

Drink water, sleep eight hours (I wish), and don't go within 400 feet of a tanning booth or I'LL SLAP YOU. HARD.

Olivia Wilde

Derive your worth from things that are truly important,

like real relationships and your relationship with yourself.

Olivia Rodrigo

> Hard work pays off. The harder you work, the more people will notice.

Sydney Sweeney

> Giving up doesn't always mean you're weak. Sometimes you're just strong enough to let go.

Taylor Swift

> Always be a first-rate version of yourself instead of a second-rate version of somebody else.

Judy Garland

> It's not your job to like me, **IT'S MINE.**

Byron Katie

> I remind myself to be kind to myself, and as slightly ridiculous as it may sound, to treat myself in the same gentle way I'd want to treat a daughter of mine. It really helps.
>
> Emma Stone

> Being comfortable in your own skin is one of the most important things to achieve. **I'm still working on it!**

— Kate Mara

I have come to realize making yourself happy is most important. Never be ashamed of how you feel. You have the right to feel any emotion you want, and do what makes you happy. **That's my life motto.**

Demi Lovato

Don't waste energy on things you can't change.

Storm Reid

Figure out who are you separate from your family, and the man or woman you're in a relationship with. Find who you are in this world and what you need to feel good alone. I think that's the most important thing in life. Find a sense of self. With that, you can do anything else.

Angelina Jolie

There's no such thing as aging, but maturing and knowledge. It's beautiful, I call that beauty.

Celine Dion

In your 20s, you're all about who you don't want to be.

In your 30s, you're asking yourself who do you want to be.

And in your 40s, you realize you just are who you are.

Amy Poehler

> I don't need the Prince Charming to have my own HAPPY ENDING.

Katy Perry

Grace Jones was an influence, because I was like, 'These shoulders! These pants! Girls can wear pants and be AWESOME.'

Lorde

Knowing you're a **BADASS BITCH** is just all what **LIFE IS ABOUT.**

Khloe Kardashian

I think no matter what you look like, the key is to first of all **be happy with yourself**. And then you know if you want to try to improve things that you don't like about yourself, then do it after you **appreciate yourself**.

Adele

> I never allow myself <u>not</u> to feel confident.

Amber Rose

People call me arrogant. I call it self-assurance I am who I am ... you like it great. You don't like it — I don't care.

Priyanka Chopra Jonas

Above all, be the heroine of your life, not the victim.

Nora Ephron

> People will stare. Make it worth their while.

Harry Winston

I am incapable of mediocrity.

Serge Gainsbourg

Too much good taste can be **VERY BORING.** Independent style, on the other hand, can be **VERY INSPIRING.**

Diana Vreeland

Self–esteem comes from being able to define the world in **your own terms** and refusing to abide by the judgement of others.

Serena Williams

I've learned to love me.
I've been like this my whole life, and I embrace me.
I love how I look.
    I am a **full woman**
and
    I'm **strong**,
and
    I'm **powerful**,
and
    I'm **beautiful**
              at the same time.

Serena Williams

One of my mantras is, 'Embrace what makes you unique, even if it makes others uncomfortable.' I keep that with me in my back pocket. Shoot, I keep it in my front pocket! I keep it in my hair.

Janelle Monae

The most beautiful thing you can wear is confidence.

Blake Lively

I was once afraid
of people saying,

> **'Who does she think she is?'**

Now I have the
courage to stand
and say,

> **'This is who I am.'**

Oprah Winfrey

> I will not let others dictate what they think my body should look like for their own comfort, **and neither should you**.

Ashley Graham

I like to think that I offer more woman per square inch.

Hannah Waddingham

I feel empowered by the fact that I can look the way that I do on stage and in photos –

I CAN LOOK THAT WAY ANY TIME I WANT.

And I feel like it's an important message to other women that they can do it, too.

Dita Von Teese

> The more you trust your intuition, the more empowered you become, the stronger you become, and the happier you become.

Giselle Bundchen

> You can knock me down but I get up twice as strong.

Lewis Hamilton

I feel like I'm ready for any dangerous situation that might come my way, provided I have a hammer on me.

Chris Hemsworth

I worked hard and made my own way, just as my father had. And just, I'm sure, as he hoped I would.

I learned, from observing him, the satisfaction that comes from striving and seeing a dream fulfilled.

Sigourney Weaver

Success?
I don't know what that word means.
I'm happy.
But success, that goes back to what in somebody's eyes success means.

For me, **success is inner peace.** That's a good day for me.

Denzel Washington

Being perfect is being flawed, accepting it and never letting it make you feel less than your best.

Jessica Alba

Take a stand for what's right. Raise a ruckus and make a change.

You may not always be popular, but you'll be part of something larger and bigger and greater than yourself.

Besides, making history is extremely cool.

Samuel L Jackson

> **Happiness is the key to success.**
>
> **If you love what you are doing, you'll be successful.**
>
> — Arnold Schwarzenegger

> **If you can't see anything beautiful in yourself, get a better mirror.**
>
> — Kendall Jenner

I love empowering women. I think it's crazy: if you're trying to belittle women, you're playing yourself – I ride with whoever rides with me.

SZA

> **If there's one thing I'm willing to bet on, IT'S MYSELF.**
>
> Beyoncé

It doesn't matter how you get knocked down in life, because that's going to happen.

All that matters is that you gotta get up.

Ben Affleck

Why are you trying so hard to fit in when you were born to stand out?

Ian Wallace

How you love yourself is how you teach others to love you.

Rupi Kaur

I
got
my
own
back.

Maya Angelou

I wanted to be an empowered woman, and I became an empowered woman. And now I want to empower every woman. And I do it through my clothes, I do it through my words, I do it through my money, I do it through everything.

Diane Von Furstenberg

> Find out who you are
> and be that person.
> Find that truth,
> live that truth,
> and everything
> else will come.

Ellen DeGeneres

> Sometimes all you need is twenty seconds of **insane courage.**

Matt Damon

Live your life as if you are already where you want to be.

Russell Simmons

Don't waste your energy trying to change opinions … Do your thing, and **don't care** if they like it.

Tina Fey

You have **no control** over other people's taste, so **focus** on staying true to your own.

Tim Gunn

Regardless of how you feel inside, always try to look like a **winner**. Even if you are behind, a sustained look of control and confidence can give you a mental edge that results in victory.

Diane Arbus

You
cannot live
to please
anyone else.

Octavia Spencer

> I used to worry about being cool. Now I realise that **I GENUINELY DON'T CARE.**

Charli XCX

The important thing is to realize that no matter what people's opinions may be, they're only just that – people's opinions.

You have to believe in your heart what you know to be true about yourself.

And let that be that.

Mary J Blige

> People are still under the illusion that every woman who is successful must be controlled by a man. **I'M THE BOSS.**

Lily Allen

Don't take yourself too seriously. Know when to laugh at yourself, and find a way to laugh at obstacles that inevitably present themselves.

Cameron Diaz

Being unique and different was a really good thing. When I walked into my agent's office for the first time, they looked at me and said,

> 'Wow, we have nobody on our books like you.'

And they signed me on my second day here.

Rebel Wilson

People will survive, and they will find happiness. Happiness only comes when you're not looking for it.

Hugh Laurie

> Find some beautiful art and admire it, and realize that that was created by human beings just like you, no more human, no less.

Maya Angelou

DO WHAT MAKES YOU FEEL GOOD. Remind yourself of what you're good at and make sure you do that.

Jessie J

I can say the one good thing is for every year where I grow up, I am kinder to myself, and I would say to the younger version of me,

'I love my body, and I have learnt to stop looking in the mirror at the things I want to change.'

Alicia Vikander

You better realize your worth and stop settling for bare minimum half ass shit.

Cardi B

Do not bring
people in your
life
who
weigh
you
down.

Michelle Obama

> **I don't want other people to decide who I am.**
>
> **I want to decide that for myself.**

Emma Watson

I taught myself confidence. When I'd walk into a room and feel scared to death, I'd tell myself, **'I'm not afraid of anybody.'** And people believed me. You've got to teach yourself to take over the world.

Priyanka Chopra Jonas

Don't let other people's opinions define who you are.

Kim Kardashian

You're doing amazing, sweetie.

Kris Jenner

> I'm not perfect. But I'll always be real.

Tupac Shakur

> I learn every day what it means to love myself, and I'm constantly figuring out what makes me feel empowered.

Hayley Williams

> There is no such thing as failure. Failure is just life trying to move us in another direction.

Oprah Winfrey

We feel a lot of pressure about looking silly or appearing weak, whatever that means, or being a failure. You have to keep in your head: **what's the worst that can happen?**

Michael Fassbender

Believe in yourself and all that you are. Know that there is something inside you that is greater than any obstacle.

Jennifer Garner

You are enough.

Unknown

> Never dull your shine for somebody else.

Tyra Banks

You have a right to the universe. You are given that right simply by being born.

Shonda Rhimes

All I need is my Chanel dress, my Louboutins, and some red lipstick.

Blake Lively

> To love oneself is the beginning of a lifelong romance.
>
> Oscar Wilde

You are bold. You are brilliant, and you are beautiful.

Ashley Graham